13

UNDERWATER DEMOLITION TEAM

WESTPAC

1969

Published by:
FindTech Ltd
P. O. Box 43698
Cleveland, OH 44143
(216) 486-4464
(877) 882-6124
www.find-tech.biz

This cruise book was originally published in 1969 after being compiled and assembled by the editors, Ltjg Peter N. Upton and PH1 (DV) Steve Waterman. At that time, less than 100 copies were printed. It is being republished to preserve the history of the document.

Although the spine says "revised by" Steven L. Waterman, only errata was corrected for this publication. "Revived" may be a more accurate term, but not an option from the Library of Congress.

Paperback ISBN: 978-0-9787637-6-3

Ebook ISBN: 978-0-9787637-5-6

Library of Congress Control Number: 2008926059

Recommissioning Day

1 July 1968

1400—UNDERWATER DEMOLITION TEAM 13 RECOMMISSIONING CEREMONY COMMENCED WITH THE PARADING OF THE COLORS CALLED FOR BY UDT-13 EXECUTIVE OFFICER LT. R. W. PETERSON. RADM. H. S. MONROE, COMPHIBTRAPAC; CAPT. BAHILL, COMPHIBPAC REPRESENTATIVE, AND CAPT. F. KAINE WERE OFFICIAL GUESTS. REMARKS WERE MADE BY RADM. MONROE AND CAPT. KAINE.

1420—UDT-13 COMMANDING OFFICER (PROSPECTIVE) LCDR. JAMES B. WILSON READ HIS ORDERS TO CAPT. KAINE TAKING COMMAND OF UDT-13 AND OFFICIALLY REPORTED UDT-13 FOR DUTY WITH NAVAL SPECIAL WARFARE GROUP PACIFIC.

1425—LT. R. W. PETERSON, EXECUTIVE OFFICER OF UDT-13, WAS AWARDED SILVER STAR BY RADM, MONROE.

1428—RECOMMISSIONING CEREMONY CONCLUDED WITH RETIRING OF THE COLORS. LIBERTY COMMENCED.

1430—THE FOLLOWING PERSONNEL ON BOARD UNDERWATER DEMOLITION TEAM THIRTEEN: LCDR. JAMES B. WILSON, COMMANDING OFFICER; LT. R. W. PETERSON, EXECUTIVE OFFICER; LT. C. C. LOMAS, LTJG SHORTT, LTJG PLUMB, LTJG HICKS, LTJG ROBERTSON, LTJG HEMMING, LTJG UPTON, LTJG THOMPSON, LTJG PODBOY, LTJG WIGGIN, LTJG GREEN, ENS TOMLIN, ENS HOLLOW, ENS JAHNCKE, BMC ATKINS, SN BAKER, HM1 BAKER, RM2 COSSE, QM3 CURLE, YN2 DE LORME, GMG2 FELTON, PR2 FLUD, BM1 GOODRICH, SN HINSON, BM3 HOLLAND, QM2 JAKUBOWSKI, SN JENKINS, ETN3 LARSEN, QM1 MACDONALD, TM1 PAYNE, BM3 SAGER, SN TANAKA, AE3 ADAME.

In Memoriam

ROBERT LEROY WORTHINGTON
CHIEF HOSPITAL CORPSMAN
UNITED STATES NAVY

Killed in action while engaged in a
SEALORDS operation,
the Duong Keo River,
Republic of Vietnam.
12 April 1969

UNDERWATER DEMOLITION
TEAM
THIRTEEN

TABLE OF CONTENTS

WESTPAC DEPLOYMENT
1969

ROSTER OF PERSONNEL

Lcdr James B. Wilson . . . . Oswego, New York
Lt Robert W. Peterson . . . . Newcastle, Pennsylvania

Lt Bruce P. Dyer . . . . Norfolk, Virginia
Ltjg George T. Green . . . . Norfolk, Virginia
Ltjg Ernest L. Jahncke, III . . . . New York City, New York
Lt Christopher C. Lomas . . . . Hamilton, New York
Ltjg James B. Lytle . . . . Bethesda, Maryland
Lt Paul B. Plumb . . . . Coronado, California
Ltjg William C. Robertson . . . . Virginia Beach, Virginia
Ltjg Peter N. Upton . . . . Buffalo, New York
Ltjg John P. Wiggin . . . . West Brookfield, Massachusetts

Seaman Stephen A. Abney . . . . San Ysidro, California
HMC Francis J. Algeo . . . . Imperial Beach, California
Seaman Michael J. Baresciano . . . . Williamstown, New Jersey
QM3 Patrick E. Broderick . . . . Sunset, Utah
Seaman Robert E. Brown . . . . Cleburn, Texas
Airman Mark A. Buland . . . . Richmond, California
ETCS Lewis C. Burger . . . . La Jolla, California
YN3 Terry P. Calhoun . . . . East Liverpool, Ohio
SM1 John G. Campbell . . . . Grass Valley, California
Seaman Peter J. Carolan . . . . Garden Grove, California
EN3 Chester K. Clark . . . . Wahiawa, Hawaii
BM3 Robert D. Clay, Jr. . . . . North Lawrence, Ohio
GMG2 Robert H. Clendening . . . . Bonfield, Illinois
MR2 Gary J. Cronin . . . . Snohomish, Washington
Seaman Philip Czerwiec . . . . Rochester, New York
YN1 Sherman L. De Lorme . . . . Cover D'Alene, Idaho
Seaman Walter G. Dudley . . . . Fernandina Beach, Florida
SM3 Marvin E. Dukes . . . . Selvyville, Delaware
BM3 Ronald S. Eaton . . . . Monroeville, Pennsylvania
RM3 Theodore R. Fager . . . . Norwalk, California
QM3 Hugh E. Freel . . . . Tawas City, Michigan
PR1 Lowell A. Flud . . . . Okmulgee, Oklahoma
SFM2 Steve L. Freed . . . . Lewistown, Pennsylvania
ABHC James H. Fricks . . . . Virginia Beach, Virginia
Seaman Brian Q. Gillen . . . . Alamogordo, New Mexico
Seaman Clarence N. Gilles . . . . Brook Park, Ohio
BUH2 Roland L. Hanson . . . . Sioux Falls, South Dakota
RD1 Clayton M. Hardman . . . . Imperial Beach, California
Seaman Forest B. Harness . . . . Lake Tahoe, California
YNSN John T. Haymaker . . . . Winchester, Virginia
GMG3 Rickey G. Hinson . . . . Fayetteville, North Carolina

QM2 William C. Jakubowski . . . . .Lackawanna, New York
GMG2 Stephen P. Jewett . . . . .Ontario, California
YN2 Peter A. Joslin . . . . .Marion, Massachusetts
Seaman Brian J. Kelly . . . . .Glendale, California
Seaman Ronald J. Kozlowski . . . . .Fairfield, Connecticut
A02 John La Borde, Jr. . . . . .Grand Bay, Alabama
MM 1 Harold Lapping, Jr. . . . . .Perkasie, Pennsylvania
ETN2 Kent A. Larsen . . . . .Coronado, California
YN2 John J. Latsko, Jr. . . . . .Cleveland, Ohio
GMG3 Ronald S. Laughery . . . . .Tempe, Arizona
Seaman Eric L. Letkemann . . . . .Denver, Colorado
MR2 Charles D. Lewis . . . . .Whittier, California
BM3 Robert W. Lewis . . . . .Toledo, Ohio
SFP2 Ephraim G. Lopez . . . . .Gypsum, Ohio
ABH3 Charles M. Long . . . . .Tonawanda, New York
SM3 Robert J. Lowry . . . . .Spokane, Washington
MMC Terry R. Manley . . . . .San Diego, California
SFP3 Brian J. Mayotte . . . . .Conoga Park, California
BM2 Steve R. McConathy . . . . .Torrance, California
Seaman William C. Morterud . . . . .Duluth , Minnesota
HM2 James W. Myers . . . . .Virginia Beach, Virginia
STG2 Arles L. Nash . . . . .St. Petersburg, Florida
ADJ2 Stanley M. Neal . . . . .Brooklyn, New York
E01 Orlin D. Nelson, Jr. . . . . .Virginia Beach, Virginia
Seaman Timothy A. Nichols . . . . .Tacoma, Washington
TM1 Coy W. Payne . . . . .Imperial Beach, California
Airman Roger L. Phillips . . . . .Terrytown, Nebraska
Seaman William R. Piper . . . . .Kansas City, Missouri
Airman William R. Pozzi . . . . .Lynnwood, California
RD3 Walter 0. Roberts . . . . .Burley, Idaho
SM3 Art "R" Ruiz . . . . .Tulare, California
BM3 Daniel F. Sager . . . . .Los Angeles, California
Seaman Michael D. Sandlin . . . . .Roosevelt, Utah
Seaman William C. Shearer . . . . .Glendale, California
PR2 Joseph A. Silver . . . . .Evansville, Indiana
Seaman Jeffrey A. Smith . . . . .Willingboro, New Jersey
QM2 Roger H. Stickle . . . . .Indianapolis, Indiana
ETN3 James W. Still . . . . .Clinton, Iowa
ETN2 Bruno P. Uberto . . . . .Pompton Lakes, New Jersey
PH1 Steven L. Waterman . . . . .South Thomaston, Maine
ABH2 Larry D. Whitehead . . . . .Talbott, Tennessee
Seaman Rodney K. Wilkerson . . . . .Newkirk, New Mexico
HM3 Lawrence C. Williams, Jr. . . . . .Fort Arthur, Texas
RM2 Kenneth T. Winter . . . . .Cumberland, Maryland

A WORD FROM THE SKIPPER

As this memorable deployment rapidly approaches its conclusion, I can't help but look back at the course of events that led us to this point: to July 1, 1968, when team THIRTEEN was reborn, and the thirty-three plankowners who initiated the process of building this organization; the months that followed as we increased in number and added to our skills. Men answered the challenge from the established Underwater Demolition Teams, ELEVEN and TWELVE. Some of us came from shore duty, others returned to the Navy from civilian life. Petty Officers who had been on duty with SEAL teams returned to duty with us, making this the first time special warfare personnel had completed the UDT/SEAL circuit. We endeavored to utilize the lengthy combat experience these men had acquired. New men fresh from basic training swelled our ranks, but the acute need for personnel still existed.

UDT TWENTY-ONE responded with an entire platoon of hand-picked volunteers. Two officers and twenty men reported to us the first week in February and for the first time since World War Two, Atlantic and Pacific Fleet Underwater Demolition Teams prepared to go into combat together.

The trans-Pacific crossing began in early February for our advanced units, and by 3 March 69 we had completed the relief of UDT ELEVEN. The past six months have brought many experiences to all of us. With the widely dispersed detachment setup, many close friends haven't seen each other since we left the strand. We know the uncertainty and fatigue of combat; some experienced the pain and agony of wounds sustained in these operations, and the separation and long periods of convalescence in hospitals. Chief Worthington, to whom this book is dedicated, made the extreme sacrifice.

Our policy of rotation enabled some to combine the relative inactivity of ECHO and FOXTROT Detachments aboard the Ready Groups with the endless miles of beach reconnaissance for Detachment BRAVO aboard the USS COOK. Detours to Hong Kong and Japan on the COOK let some enjoy the liberty accorded other Seventh Fleet units. Some of you were busy adding to the annals of underwater demolition with your combat demolition techniques in Dets DELTA, GOLF, and HOTEL, and others were busy rewriting the techniques of reconnaissance on Det CHARLIE with the TUNNY.

The tempo of daily operations that we have sustained since our arrival in March has demanded a 100% effort from all of us.

Underwater demolition has always been an area where exceptional effort is accepted as standard, but the tremendous job you have all done, often under adverse conditions, is one we can all be proud of.

My bias leads me to conclude that this was the most active and productive deployment by an Underwater Demolition Team in any period since World War Two.

James B. Wilson,
Commanding

6

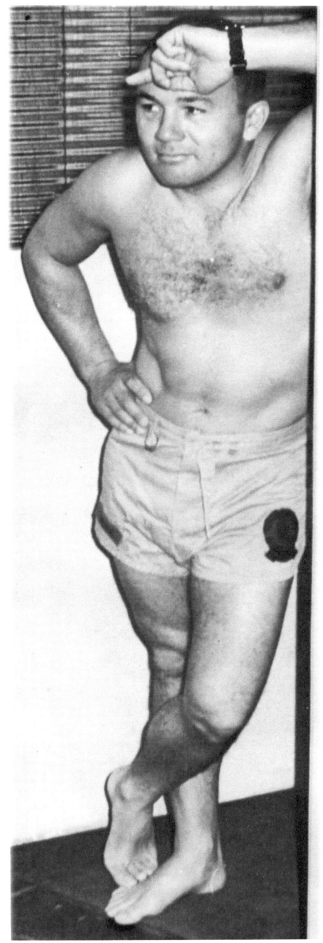

ABOUT THE XO

Lt. Robert Peterson reported to UDT THIRTEEN from combat duty in Vietnam with SEAL TEAM TWO. A native of Newcastle, Pa., he received his commission from OCS in Newport, R.I. in 1961. Upon graduation from Underwater Demolition Team Training in Little Creek, Lt. Peterson was assigned to SEAL TWO and the Special Operations Group in Vietnam. The XO then served as First Lieutenant aboard the Guided Missile Frigate LEAHY. Returning to SEAL TWO in 1966 for action in Vietnam, Lt. Peterson was awarded the Silver Star for heroism in the Mekong Delta.

The XO currently makes his home in Chula Vista, California with his wife, Karen, and their son.

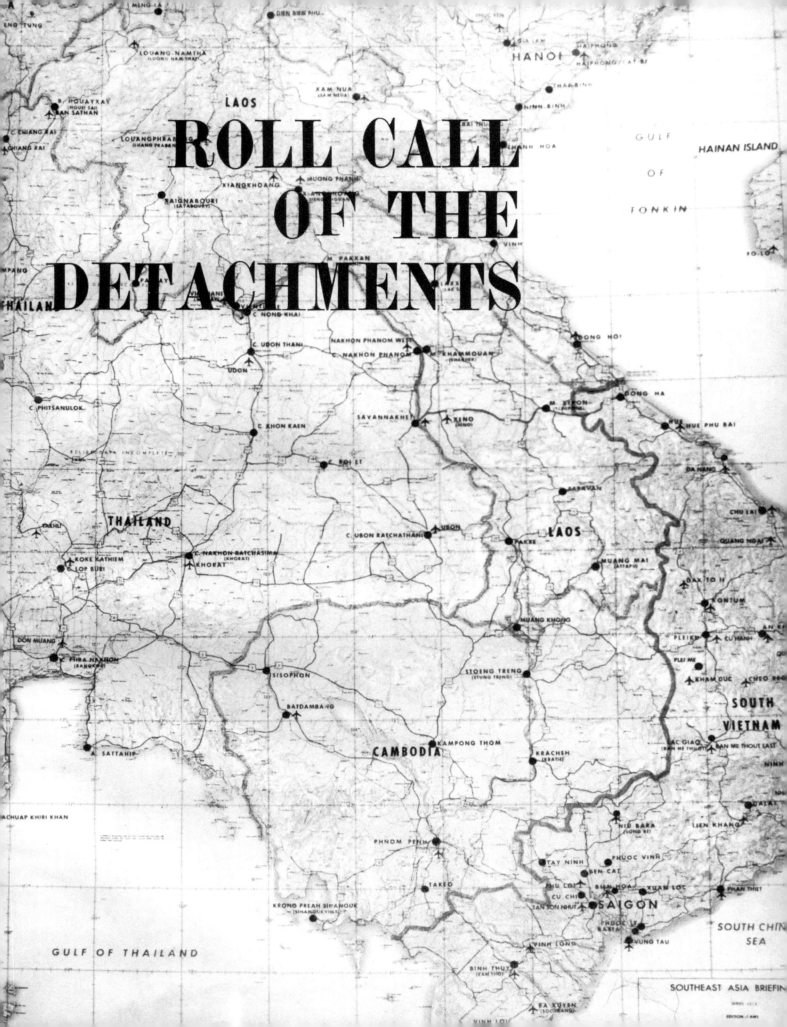

ROLL CALL OF THE DETACHMENTS

The nucleus of UDT THIRTEEN WESTPAC, Det ALFA, is located aboard the Naval Station in Subic Bay, Republic of the Philippines. This headquarters element consists of the Skipper, the XO, plus eight to twelve departmental personnel charged with maintenance, logistics, and administrative support of the operating detachments. Long days are the routine; long nights can be the reward. UDT THIRTEEN'S Chief Master-at-Arms, MMC Terry Manley, describes the Subic scene.

Under-staffed and overworked could well be the phrase used to describe Detachment ALFA. From reveille until 0700 muster, things are somewhat normal, but immediately after quarters, things begin to happen. Monday and Wednesday from 0700 'til 0800, all hands are involved in PT and a two and one-half mile run. Tuesday and Thursday, water polo is played by all hands until 0800. Friday, weather permitting, we in Det ALFA take to the air to try out Flud's and Silver's parachutes and log as many jumps as possible. In the event of bad weather, we once again use PT or water polo to fill in for the jump.

It is here in Det ALFA that maintenance and upkeep are performed on all operating equipment, with a large amount of this upkeep falling on the diving department. Here we also screen future UDT trainees and pass the results of this screening along to Phibpac.

Our weekly schedule tends to lean heavily on training and instruction of personnel in Det ALFA. This, along with the PT and water polo, makes for a pretty well-rounded schedule for those of us that are here in Subic Bay.

By
MMC Terry Manley

Holiday routine at White Rock Beach.

Squad leader De Lorme. 175 pounds of tiger meat, leads his Remington firing line through the daily rigors of paper warfare.

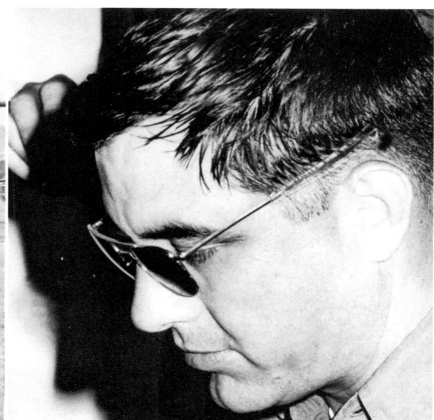

"Lt" Neal does one of his many things, screening prospective UDT candidates.

Flud ponders the watch bill.

Knowledge.

13

Riggers Flud and Silver journeyed to Fort Magsaysay, north of Manila, for two days of jump instructing with our Filipino counterpart, Underwater Operations Unit.

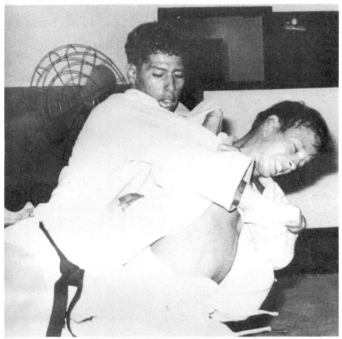

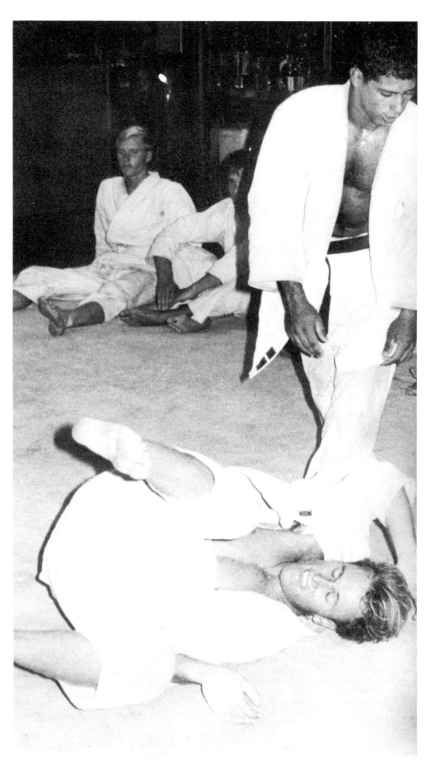

We utilized the talents of black-belter Stephen Wojtowicz for combatives training in Subic. Some of us were rewarded with five weeks of intensive work at the Kodokan, in Tokyo—a first for UDT.

15

MR2 Cronin demonstrates Flud's easy-to-follow, 7-step method for *in extremis* deployment of the reserve parachute.

Left leg strap, sergeant!

Jumpers en route.

Stand in the door...
...GO!

The drop zone at Castillejos was a curious blend of rocks, elephant grass, irrigation ditches, bright-eyed children, sleepy-eyed water buffalo... and the tee, for those who managed to find it.

Where angels tread.

AIRBORNE! and A-OK.

Any jump you walk away from is a good jump.

17

The First Special Forces Group, located at Camp Hardy, Okinawa, had a surprise or two in store for those of us who thought the 24-hour training day went out of style with UDTRA. LtCol Happersett and Captain Fox concocted a 'UDT special' for team THIRTEEN, including night IBS paddles, lengthy 'nature walks' through the mountainous jungle terrain, special demolitions and weapons work, rappelling, plus pathfinder training.

"Twice during the lull in beach surveys, Det BRAVO had the opportunity to attend Special Forces training on Okinawa. Their commanding officer, a gentlemanly lieutenant colonel, reminded us that physical fitness doesn't disappear with youth and that there are many reasons, besides insomnia, for not being able to sleep. His school and his night problems for one. After completion of the course, we took an evening in town for a different sort of night life," says Ltjg Wiggin.

Team THIRTEEN reciprocated with pleasure, conducting SCUBA-familiarization courses in Subic for thirteen of the Green Beret instructors. Their training included bounce dives, compass swims, and the ever-thrilling IBS cast and recovery.

Both special warfare units benefited tremendously from this exchange program, each garnering additional skills while obtaining a deep appreciation for the other's capabilities.

The skipper is a hard charger.

Our early morning wake-up sessions in the pool or on the PT field provided more than ample opportunity for us to sweat out the previous evening's ration of San Miguel.

20

Second-class Divers School provided us with a new capability.

The 'blood and guts' or the 'join the Navy and see the world' Detachment, BRAVO, embarked aboard the USS COOK, LPR–130, conducted extensive beach survey work in the Republic of Vietnam. This mission, involving the charting of beach soundings out to 30 feet, shoreline features, and significant hazards to navigation, lies at the heart of UDT, the kind of job she was designed to perform.

During the never-forgotten days of training in either Coronado or Little Creek, a 35-lane beach reconnaissance was considered unendurable and could be counted on to produce moanings, groanings, teeth-chattering, and gun-decking from the weary tadpoles. Yet a working day aboard the COOK finds the UDT THIRTEEN swimmer line kicking, stroking, lead-line bobbing, and gliding through an average of 175 beach lanes, each 25 yards wide. The near-crystalline, emerald hued 85° water has kept the troopers happy and toasty warm for upward of 5 solid hours.

"When your lead line is giving you your 84th twelve-foot sounding in a row and there are still 4 miles of beach to go, and our technology has just put two men on the moon, you begin to wonder if perhaps there might be a better way," writes Ltjg Wiggin.

Our WESTPAC grand total: over 60 miles of beach surveyed, often performed in less-than-pleasant weather and surf conditions, and always under the threat of encountering hostile fire. Rewards were commensurate with the arduous job, however, as the COOK managed visits to Hong Kong, Singapore, Okinawa, Japan, Formosa, the Philippines, and of course, Vietnam. Lt. Paul Plumb records his impressions.

The first group assigned to Det BRAVO, our beach reconnaissance element in WESTPAC, known as "Plumb's Plunderers," put forth three months of operations into the hydrographic survey and cartography of more than thirty-one miles of South Vietnamese beach. The successful completion of our assigned 25 beaches involved the coordination and cooperation between our entire detachment and the USS COOK. The COOK acted as our home away from Subic for the two officers and seventeen enlisted that normally made up BRAVO.

In many cases, on the beaches to be surveyed, enemy disposition was unknown. On other beaches, both Viet Cong and NVA elements were known to have operated in the area. It was the Unknown and the Uncertain that made each survey a unique challenge.

Prior to setting out on any beach, we established liaison with all available supporting units. Many times swiftboat or Coast Guard patrol boat coverage were all that could be obtained. On three occasions, however, the U.S. Army supported us with a platoon of ground troops. In most cases, however, our only beach defense perimeter support was provided by our own armed personnel. It was our own security who detected two Viet Cong ambushes in one day. Steve Nash and Charlie Lewis spotted the enemy positions and warned the beach party, thus allowing for rapid withdrawal. Both beaches were cleared of the enemy, allowing for subsequent completion of the surveys.

Much of the success of BRAVO should be attributed to the ready and willing support of the USS COOK'S personnel and her outstanding skipper, Lcdr Bruce Tager. Ranging from the all important supply of combat information provided from CIC, to the mess cooks, support from the COOK was beyond reproach, always first class.

The hard work and extra effort of the chartmakers Hugh 'Pig' Freel, Mark 'Twigman' Buland, Ted Fager, Scott Laughery, and Brian 'Mad-Dog' Kelly played one of the central parts in completing our job successfully.

Also, we cannot forget any of the following: the sore right arm of Bill 'The Lung' Pozzi trying to keep his outboard engine going; Steve 'It's a lonely feeling' Nash and Charles 'How I hate the soft sand' Lewis at beach security; Steve 'Waterpump' Waterman and his 18 Nikonos; Ernest 'Torch' Jahncke trying to follow orders; Mel "Squeeze" Hardman at compressing the able bodies into our compartment aboard the COOK. We loved them one and all.

By
Lt Paul Plumb

AMBUSHED NEAR DANANG

On 27 June, 1969, a Viet Cong Squad initiated a fierce small arms and automatic weapons ambush which resulted in the medevac of the first BRAVO casualty in recent history, SA Ronald J. Kozlowski, wounded as a bullet tore through his left forearm.

From his vantage in the swimmer line, Seaman Jerry Dudley summarizes the action.

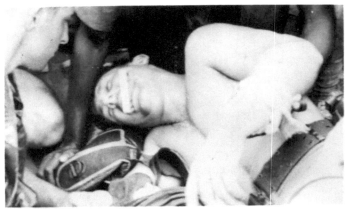

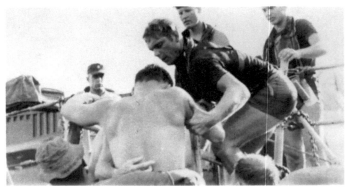

The briefing was no different than any we'd had before. Everyone was prepared for the standard admin recon with the minimum number of personnel in the beach party. The day had started like every other day: early preparation, muster on the fantail, man the Mark IV boat, then move in on one of the beach flanks. Little did we know our recon would be halted in mid-stream, a man wounded before its completion.

It began as the COOK'S small boat, manned by the UDT beach party, moved in to the right flank of the beach and put the men ashore. First on land were the three security men: Lewis as forward, Hanson as middle, and McConathy as rear. Next went the range pole men, Baresciano on the front flag, and Kozlowski on the rear. Last to leave the boat were Gillen, the beach cartographer, and Ltjg Wiggin, the beach OIC. Weaponry for the beach party consisted of M-16 rifles and M-79 grenade launchers.

The beach party landed without complications. The perimeter security set, range poles were lined up and the swimmer line was put into the water. I was number two swimmer, 50 yards from shore.

The recon was running quite smoothly until the 15th lane when all hell broke loose. We were hit by small arms fire

not 50 yards from where our beach party had landed. The swimmers submerged and headed for sea, while the beach party hit the deck. Our security began returning fire, followed immediately by the big .50 cal guns on our support boats. The air was full of lead, and no one wanted to pop his head up for a decent target. Suddenly a member of the beach party, Kozlowski, sprang up into a low crouch and began to sprint the necessary few yards to enter the water. Just as he rose, a round caught him in the forearm, entering the top and ripping out the bottom side. The man screamed: "Ouwieee!! Medic!" and then attempted to swim to sea. Mr. Wiggin was beside him, in the water, in a matter of seconds. He pulled the wounded man's life vest and then his own. Others in the beach party who had gradually crawled back into the water, and the surrounding swimmers from the swimmer line, closed in on the wounded frog and aided in assuring his survival. The small boat, which at this time was filling the hillside with its firepower, was summoned to the wounded man by swimmers using the UDT distress signal, a hand waved over the head. Swiftly, the coxswain moved his craft to the group of men and picked up, first, the wounded Kozlowski, then the remainder of the beach party, myself, and the other members of the swimmer line.

The remainder of the swimmer line was picked up farther out at sea by the Mark IV, which had, only minutes before, caught a round on the starboard side. The bullet had passed through the boat 18 inches above the waterline and travelled farther on, entering the medical kit of our corpsman. As the Mark IV was the faster of the two boats, the wounded man was transferred to it from the other support boat, an LCPR, and then rushed to the USS COOK and given further medical treatment. He was later flown to DaNang by medevac helo for surgery.

It wasn't long before the enemy was suppressed and driven away. Once again UDT moved into the beach to complete, this time unchallenged, the assignment we had been given.

By
Seaman Jerry Dudley

CHARLIE

Ltjg Green and Seaman Abney relay these thoughts on Det CHARLIE, whose scope of operations remains classified:

"Det Charlie's activities during the early weeks of this deployment were, at best, minimal. Plagued by 'tired' equipment and a 'sluggish' resupply system, the Minimariners (to coin a term) did well to accomplish the requisite training prior to boarding the TUNNY. The Subic training period was primarily intended to tie together loose ends and put to a practical use the invaluable training bestowed upon us during 10 weeks of stateside instruction.

...Det CHARLIE is like any other detachment in the way that it hardly ever has two operations that are the same. Each operation has something a little different than the others ... preparing the SDV is the most important part ... parts have to be checked before and after any operation. Chief Burger was in charge of this important area. Roberts also did a great deal in the maintenance field...

Thanks are in order to the officers and crew of the TUNNY whose co-operation and professionalism made our stay with them a pleasurable experience...."

RD3 "Mole" Roberts descends from the TUNNY'S escape trunk, making him the last UDT swimmer to do so. The TUNNY was decommissioned during Team 13's cruise, removing the gallant lady from the roles of active duty.

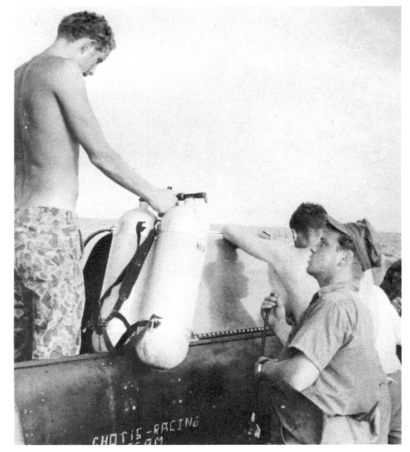

THE DELTA

From the fertile heartland of the Mekong Delta, Ltjg John Wiggin relays information concerning UDT Detachment HOTEL'S operations with the Mobile Riverine Force. The MRF concept revolves around the transporting of Army 9th Infantry Division combat troops by armored Navy river boats, which penetrate deeply into the tributaries of the Mekong River, for troop insertions. Seven ship-size Naval units, anchored in the wide expanse of the main river, provide support for the entire operation.

During the spring and early summer months of 1969, large portions of the riverine squadrons were transferred to the Vietnamese. This equipment turnover was reflected in HOTEL'S sharply decreased tempo of operations during May and June, and resulted in the ultimate removal of UDT personnel from the 'Green Fleet' in July. Ltjg Green and four others, supported by Winter and Meyers, kept station in the Delta area for test and evaluation of a swimmer detection system near Saigon. Ltjg Robertson and the remaining enlisted personnel from HOTEL flew to DaNang for work with swiftboats and SEATIGER riverine operations.

ALFA's and TANGO'S move into battle —

The scheduled drawdown of the Mobile Riverine Force in July, great, but damn, it's taking our HOTEL. Thus the MERCER, our USS HILTON, is going home for redeployment. Seeing that our det down here has been split up, guess I'll pack up and maybe move in with the rest of the frogs down river on the APL-30, not the Hotel Ritz in its own right, but luxurious in comparison with life elsewhere.

And they're turning over the smaller riverine support boats, too—to the Vietnamese. We're all wondering what's in store for us. It surely has been slowing down for us since summer; summer by the calendar, not by the heat. Maybe this latest change was the reason.

But the boats, damn they were slow. The Five Horsemen of the Apocalypse running on a muddy track: Alfa, Tango, Charlie, Mike, and Zippo. Mudders all! But powerful; carrying the most diabolical array of weaponry from small arms to 105 howitzer and flame. And well-armored.

The ops were more extended than at other dets. Five of us would hop aboard a Tango boat for at least a week, and that would be home for the duration. With the crew and us would be our gear, our food, our weapons, and piles of ammunition and explosives if we were lucky; twenty U.S. Army combat troops if we weren't. Add mud in either case.

If no one else presents an "Ode to the Mud", we in the Delta sure would like to. Peanut butter will stick to your ribs as you swallow it; the mud will stick there because that's how deep it is. And for laughs let's have mud blowing in your eyes at the same time. Never saw a fat Vietnamese, did you? The mud affords any fat ones a wonderful course in natural selection.

Our ops were usually demolitions: blowing bunkers, fighting positions, sampans, tunnels, and booby traps. On occasion, we'd clear river obstacles or conduct salvage operations on sunken river craft or downed helos. On our searches for submerged arms caches, we accounted for three tons of enemy ammunition. Hull checks for enemy mines were routine as were clearing of ship's screws that fouled in fishnets. And where the streams were narrow and the meanders frequent, with Charlie lying by or suspected of being so, we participated in a bit of preventive maintenance by preparing the river banks first with intensive fire. If the Viet Cong ever fired first, we'd return that fire a hundredfold.

And let us not forget the My Tho massage cortege. . .

By
Ltjg John P. Wiggin

DANANG

DaNang remains the focal point for UDT personnel attached to Detachments ECHO, FOXTROT, and HOTEL. The team facility, located at Camp Tein Sha and affectionately dubbed "Frogsville," functions as a joint barracks/chow hall/ recreation center for these in-country dets. More often than not, however, ECHO and FOXTROT are embarked aboard ships serving the Amphibious Ready Groups (ARG's), waiting, waiting, waiting,… for operational commitments which would send them into long-anticipated action. Ltjg Ernest Jahncke's dialogue illuminates this bad dream.

Det HOTEL, reassigned in July from work in the Mekong Delta, tips the opposite scale, performing intensively and admirably in SEATIGER swiftboat river operations, similar in nature and scope to the SEALORDS operations in the Ca Mau peninsula. Ltjg W. C. Robertson describes the action.

DANANG AND SEATIGER

In-country R&R center for the ARG's, gedunker's heaven, and beer capital of DaNang. Yes sir! 'This is Frogsville, where UDT detachments live and play. Hazardous duty here originally consisted of bottom searches, clearing screws, surveying the admiral's landing site, and opening beer cans. Add fried rice, volleyball, no air conditioning, and you'll have DaNang. Be forewarned: leave the flies, cockroaches, and rats strictly alone, for they live and eat here, too. Thus passed the pre-swiftboat days.

The DaNang rut was bridged, however, when we began operating with Coastal Division TWELVE. Soon thereafter, Frogsville got its first combat detachment assigned to task group 115.1, or SEATIGER. Finally, after playing landscape artist and receiving the Gold Seal from Better Homes and Gardens, UDT put down their shovels and rakes… and beer cans (empty), and picked up their weapons to answer the call.

It was sheer pleasure to finally participate, and the swiftboats enjoyed us as much as we enjoyed working for them. The small Det HOTEL, made up of one officer and four enlisted, was confronted with many jobs, all of which were interesting and varied. We reconned the inland waters of rivers and bays, blew bridges, and perhaps most demandingly, rode the river craft in search of water obstacles, enemy bunkers, weapons caches, and the enemy himself. Most of our operations found us in the Cui Dai River, which is twenty kilometers south of DaNang. As our SEATIGER ops increased, we began working closely with the Explosive Ordnance Disposal Teams and had an enjoyable work-hard, play-hard relationship with them.

Just a word of thanks and congratulations to the men of this detachment for their outstanding professionalism and spirit—a 4.0 job.

By
Ltjg W. C. Robertson

40

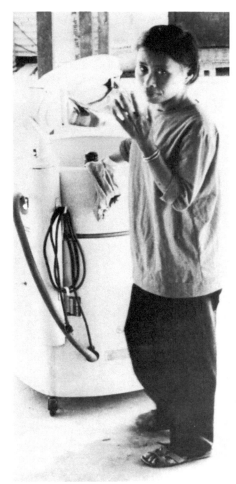

THE ARG SCENE

UDT THIRTEEN'S unflappable frogs, assigned to the ARG's, spent no small part of their substantial energies trying to get off and stay off various LSD's operating with the Ready Groups, in order to operate out of Frogsville, DaNang. The dialogue would often go something like this:

Mr. Jahncke: "Listen up, guys! I just got word that the Commodore wants us back on the USS ALAMO in three hours. Get your gear together. I want you ready in two hours."

GMG2 Jewett: "How long will we be out there steaming in circles this time?"

Mr. Jahncke: "I don't know. There's a pending operation in the next few days, so shouldn't be too long."

BUH2 Hanson: "I'm not EVEN going back out on that barge to sit on my butt and do nothing day after day."

Jewett: "I guess that gives me about two hours to finish getting drunk."

Three days later, aboard the ALAMO:

Seaman Nichols: "Mr. Jahncke, what happened to this pending op?"

Mr. Jahncke: "I don't know and neither does the Operations Officer. The last I heard, it's still pending. Where's Carolan? He's late for PT."

RD3 Roberts: "He's probably locked himself in the ship's library or something."

Hanson: "I'm not EVEN about to stay on this ship for another week."

Six days later. Scene: the same:

Jewett: "Mr. Jahncke, why don't you tell the Commodore that we have more important commitments in DaNang?"

Mr. Jahncke: "The Commodore says we're committed to him, but I'm taking the admin helo over to find out when we can get off."

And, the next day:

Jewett: "When are we getting off, Mr. Jahncke?"

Mr. Jahncke: "Maybe in three or four days when the ship goes to DaNang."

Hanson: "Maybe! I'm not EVEN about to stay on here any longer. Why can't we get a helo to take us in?"

Seaman Clay: "Because we're doing PT on the flight deck all the time."

Finally, three days later, in DaNang Harbor, still aboard the ALAMO:

Jewett: "Well, are we going to get off today, Mr. Jahncke?"

Mr. Jahncke: "Maybe, I don't know. I'll have to check with the Operations Officer-something about a pending op."

Nichols: "Maybe!... That's all we ever get out of you!"

Thus it went: the never-ending struggle to get ashore in DaNang. And, believe this, Dets ECHO and FOXTROT did actually spend much more time ashore in DaNang that had ever been the case with Teams ELEVEN and TWELVE.

By
Ltjg Ernest Jahncke

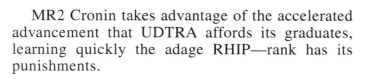

MR2 Cronin takes advantage of the accelerated advancement that UDTRA affords its graduates, learning quickly the adage RHIP—rank has its punishments.

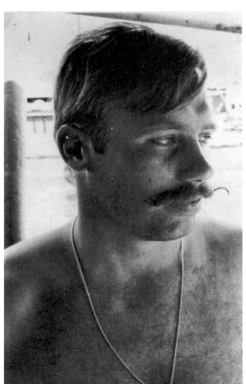

GOLF

The southern tip of Vietnam is charted as a blue-green mass. This region encompasses the Ca Mau peninsula, characterized by dense mangrove foliage, impassable marshland, and a vast system of waterways ranging in size from the Cua Lon River, at points 600 meters wide, to minute three-foot canals.

Recent involvement in SEALORDS riverine operations in this area marked the first time since Korean War demolition raids that an underwater demolition team has taken an active, aggressive role as a component of a combat task force. The SEALORDS concept integrated PCF swiftboat units, MSF or RF/PF (Mobile Strike Force or Regional and Popular Force) indigenous ground troops, LHFT (Navy 'Seawolf' light helicopter fire teams) with UDT. The force utilized UDT's swimming and demolition capabilities in efforts to curb the Viet Cong insurgency in regions previously considered his sanctuary.

The swiftboat-a 50 foot aluminum-hulled patrol craft, first introduced into riverine warfare in 1967. A daring transit of the Cua Lon River by a curious unit proved the feasibility of such operations and led to the development of the SEALORDS concept.

Sweep and Destroy missions along the rivers and treacherous canals were conducted by a joint PCF/UDT/MSF/LHFT Task Force. Results were always positive as we found either the enemy or his implements of war.

A DAY ON THE
SONG ONG DOC

This day starts as a faint reddish glow in the East; the sun, beholder of all things, slowly ascends to its own width above the featureless horizon.

Yet, even before the first rays of sun are pouring forth from the heavens, there is a hustle and bustle about the decks of the USS TERRELL COUNTY as members of UDT 13 Detachment GOLF prepare their equipment and weapons for the day's operation on the banks of the Song Ong Doc in the Ca Mau Peninsula. The engines of the swiftboats throb to life with a throaty roar as the men climb down the cargo nets to them. Weapons, demolitions, flak jackets, C-rations, and other equipment are passed down to the people who are already on the decks of the boats. As the lines are cast off and the aluminum-hulled craft head shoreward through the grey shroud of morning mist, there is a seeming lack of conversation among the men. Most words are not of the mission at hand, but are of insignificant trivialities, as a pack of cigarettes owed a friend, or the quality of the morning meal.

Shortly, the craft reach the rendezvous point and several junks come alongside. They unload their detachments of Popular Forces Troops and make their way back into the gloom of early morning.

By the time the swifts reach the mouth of the Song One Doc, the sun is casting its warmth over the already tepid swamps and the air has been cleared of all signs of night.

Apprehension grows as the boats begin their trek up the winding river; the men who haven't already donned their flak jackets and helmets now do so. Each man checks his weapon carefully and insures that he has sufficient ammunition at hand in case of any combat eventuality. The coxswains rev up the twin diesels and the boats begin to gather the necessary speed to permit rapid evasive maneuvers in case of ambush.

Dozens of sets of eyes scan the shoreline on either side of the river as the boats steadily cut wakes through the turbid river water. Even though seeing nothing, the mind is still allowed to assess the possibility of a massive, well-organized ambush, just lying in wait for the first boat that comes along. The thoughts of these men are known only by their owners. For fleeting moments, as if by some sort of combat-induced mental telepathy, there is rapport among the troops. Cold stare is met by cold stare. All are wondering, "Jesus Christ. I wonder if they'll hit us this time."

Suddenly, as if right on cue, several spouts of water roar skyward and the shock of the explosions can be felt through the decks of the boats. Automatic weapons on the shore open fire with the staccato rhythm that is so familiar to all who know the AK-47. Rounds are hitting all around the boats and the already burdened engines are called on for a few more RPM's to get the boats hurriedly out of the kill zone. The 50s on the swifts are steadily hosing the riverbank in the area of the enemy's positions. To insure of no successful attempt at a crossfire, one or two guns are directed across the river at the opposite bank. M-79 grenades are sent arcing toward the suspected offensive bunkers and, as the boats head in to beach, the troops remove flak jackets and pick up weapons and ammo for the insertion. As soon as the boat bows touch the soft mud of the riverbank, the troops are off and spreading out to sweep the bank and outflank the enemy, cutting him off from all possibility of escape to the hinterland. There, he would be almost impossible to find.

Structures afforded sanctuary to the enemy and were burned.

As the UDT personnel slog across a small stream, there is a burst of automatic weapon's fire that rakes the bushes and trees around them. No one is hit and they move forward toward the enemy's position. Continuous fire is poured at the VC positions from M-16s, M-79s, and M-60s. A few of the PF troops are sporadically shooting their M-2 carbines in the general direction of the enemy. Without warning two explosions are heard to the rear of the position held by the UDT personnel. Two B-40 rockets had been fired by the VC, but they were luckily aimed too high.

One UDT man, armed with an M-60 machine gun and about 500 rounds of ammo, is seen moving ahead and to the right of the other troops. As soon as he is within 50 yards of the VC position, he opens fire on their hiding place in the bushes. The shrubbery is seen moving to one side of his position and another man shouts this information to the machine gunner, who immediately directs his fire at the base of the bushes in question.

By this time, the PFs and the rest of the UDT personnel have moved around to the left of the shrubs and all of them advance forward in a line. They move less than 20 yards when one of the PFs locates a VC body. Fifteen yards away, another is found and near them lie an AK-47, the barrel still hot, and several B-40 rockets and their launcher.

Stream and canal crossings were refreshing but short-lived, due to the extreme vulnerability of the patrol to enemy fire.

Light helo fire teams provided air coverage for the insertion-extraction phases, often hitting targets of opportunity with their 2.75-inch rockets and M-60 fire.

Meanwhile, the Seawolf helicopters are overhead, cutting off all possible escape routes with accurate rocket strikes and deadly machine gun fire from their M-60 flex guns and door gunners. Across a small canal, more Viet Cong ambushers meet their doom at the hands of the PFs and their U.S. Army advisors.

The area is secured as much as possible and the troops move along the riverbank to the point where the ambush took place. As they plod wearily through the knee-deep mud, a series of freshly-dug bunkers, a shovel, and a pair of wires are found running into the water. Inside one of the bunkers, a small bamboo frame containing a dozen flashlight batteries hooked in series gives the hint that all of the explosions on the river weren't rockets, and that one of them must have been a water mine that was command-detonated from this bunker.

The bunkers are systematically destroyed with demolitions, as are the captured rockets. A small sampan found in the canal is destroyed in a rapid manner with a concussion grenade.

The swifts have now moved in to the banks and the troops commence loading aboard in an orderly manner with several men watching to the rear of the extraction for any signs of an attempt at another attack.

Lewis fires his M-60 into a Viet Cong sniping position.

Extraction—at low tides, slow, cumbersome, and wet.

The troops are safely on board and the engines are backed down. Mud is seen to swirl up from the river bottom as the craft move out from the bank. As the boats move in line down the river, the men are still intently watching the riverbanks. The danger is not over. There is still the possibility of another attack, but none comes.

The PFs are let off the boats at their village and all the little kids in the world come down to greet the boats and try to bum candy and cigarettes from the Americans. The boats leave the village and head back to sea where they will tie up alongside the TERRELL COUNTY for the night. The crews and UDT people will eat, sleep, clean weapons, and prepare to go out again tomorrow.

By
PH1 (DV) Steve Waterman

52

Captured Booty—a recoilless rifle and Chinese made AK-47 assault rifle.

Ubiquitous, stultifying mud, usurper of all reasonable expectations for orderly progress in any direction except down.

A log and mud bunker position is eliminated in a demonstration of "overkill."

The detonating wires leading into this massive mine were discovered during a troop sweep along the Bay Hap River. UDT attempted to blow the device from shore, with negative results. The wires were then checked for booby trapping. Determined safe, UDT hauled the mine to shore by the leads.

Water mines: a source of danger on all river transits.

One of Madame Nhu's charcoal kilns receives a face lift along the Cua Lon River.

The mine was blown sympathetically, using six pounds of plastic explosive. The blast spumed 150 feet into the air.

Booby-traps—the deadly hazards to land navigation which account for over half of all ground casualties in the Mekong Delta regions.

The boss contemplating the crossing.

DEATH OF THE 43

Between the hours of 1800-1900, 12 April 1969, at a well-camouflaged sector along the narrow Duong Keo, southernmost in South Vietnam's vast system of navigable waterways, U.S. Navy PCFs ("swiftboats"), then supporting Vietnamese Marine river operations under the aegis of SEALORDS, incurred their most devastating and demoralizing setback to date. A well-planned and perfectly-executed Viet Cong heavy-weapons ambush inflicted heavy material damage to every swiftboat unit involved in the action. It accounted for thirty-nine wounded in action, many seriously injured, requiring immediate medical evacuation. Vietnamese Marine casualties were of equal severity.

One of the eight boats involved, PCF 43, was totally destroyed during the encounter. Its mangled, blackened carcass still rests on the ambush site, a somewhat grotesque sepulchre and testament to the forlorn events of that bitter hour. Of her seventeen embarked Navymen, including ten members of Underwater Demolition Team THIRTEEN Detachment GOLF and one SEALORDS staff officer, two were killed: Ltjg Don Droz, the boat OIC, and HMC Robert Worthington, the UDT corpsman. Only three of the remaining fifteen escaped unscathed. UDT wounded in action include SM3 Art Ruiz, Seaman Michael Sandlin, SM3 Robert Lowry, Seaman William Piper, GMG3 Rickey Hinson, and Ltjg Peter Upton.

Ltjg Upton's story revolves around the thoughts and actions of those fifteen and is intended to stand as a tribute to their raw courage, a reflection of their brute will to survive.

Vietnamese mornings are singularly beautiful and manifest a stark antithesis to the rather brutal fact that the country is pervaded by deprivation and the ravaging of war. The morning of 12 April was true to that idyllic form: a typical golden-hued glimmer emanating from the pastelled east suffusing into the mellow radiance of the silvery west as the sun and moon exchanged benign glances, then gracefully parted. However, this morning elegance passed quickly, blending into the searing heat of early afternoon, when word was passed to UDT promulgating the *modus operandi* and logistics requirements for the upcoming three-day SEALORDS operation. Lusty grunting supplemented the detachment's more basic four-letter vocabulary as personal gear, weapons, "C" rations, and over eight hundred pounds of high explosives were then transferred from the tank stowage deck of the WESCHESTER COUNTY, LST 1167, onto the fantail of the PCF 43, assigned to support UDT for the day. It was about 1630 hours when UDT personnel scampered down the sagging cargo net, consummating the already bulking load.

Rendezvous with the PCF units involved in the mission took place approximately one hour later, one thousand meters outside the gaping mouth of the Duong Keo, the watery path which would lead to the day's assigned sweep area. Forty-three informed the command boat of her special cargo, then took her assigned station as the rear element of a stately file of eight units. Flak gear was donned and battle stations manned on the fantail as the boats proceeded to enter the foreboding jaws of this river, infamous for its demonstrated hostility to allied units who dared venture into her inner reaches.

On this day a Viet Cong heavy weapons company, consisting of approximately seventy-five hard-core guerrillas, was located in the area of the Duong Keo when they received warning through an elaborately contrived signal system that a swiftboat incursion was under way. A well-fortified sector, up the river about five kilometers, interlaced with freshly-built bunker, trench, and spider-hole emplacements and permeated with thick mangrove vegetation, provided excellent cover for their weapons positions. Almost guaranteed of success, the enemy set up and waited.

…Discipline was perfect: the Viet Cong patiently awaited the greatest possible number of boats to be encompassed in their kill zone, then triggered the ambush with a claymore mine aimed at the lead boat. All hell broke loose as a murderous fusillade of rocket, recoilless rifle, machine gun, and small arms fire ensued. Every boat in the file received immediate hits and personnel casualties, but each roared back with her full arsenal of heavy .50 caliber machine guns. One by one the boats maneuvered upstream, out of enemy range, seeking open ground on which to set up an emergency medical evacuation station.

PCF 43 never made it. Her position as last unit in the file, aggravated by her heavy load, combined to seal her doom. For, as the lead boats were exiting the kill zone and scrambling to safety upstream, the 43 was just arriving; as the first seven boats churned and leapt forward in violent reaction, throttles to the wall, the 43 succumbed to her bulk, falling farther and father behind until she was relatively alone, hopelessly alienated in the center of the kill zone.

Viet Cong gunners then focused on the hapless intruder. Singled out for the kill, the 43 was ripped asunder, inexorably, and with lightning-like quickness: cascading water spouts signalled the near misses, though gunners at point-blank range will miss but once. One B-40 rocket found the fantail, instantly killing Doc Worthington. Hinson and Piper received frag wounds from the blast, Piper's helmet perforated and blown off by a piece of shrapnel. AK-47 rounds raked the deck, one

piercing Sandlin's left leg, leaving a clean, though gaping, wound. Another rocket exploded in the pilot house, mortally wounding the OIC and knocking the coxswain unconscious for precious seconds. Naked, without a guiding hand, 43 gesticulated wildly and careened into the north bank of the river, coming to her final, alien rest, high and dry amidst the mangrove foliage directly in front of the Viet Cong emplacements.

The bewildering, awesome reality of the situation was beclouded by momentary shock. The enemy, probably in a similar state of amazement, did not organize directly and afforded the 43's survivors invaluable minutes in which to orient themselves. Lt. Lomas scurried into the pilot house and aided the wounded there. Sandlin's pain was eased by a quick shot of morphine and a battle dressing. The sporadic shrapnel wounds of a minor nature were of no immediate concern. Survival, and survival only, was paramount, and to live, the survivors knew they had to fight. To this end, a hasty defense perimeter was formed. Campbell, with Piper and Broderick on the fantail, maintained constant M-79 grenade fire into the north bank. Luckily, the 43 boat canted toward the river and provided some natural cover for them. Crew members, discarding the .50 caliber weapons as useless, grabbed M-16 rifles and set up firing positions covering the south bank, thereby providing the stricken unit with a 360 degree perimeter.

Simultaneously with these actions, Ruiz and Lowry found the detachment's M-60 machine gun, and, using the 43's hull for cover, slid past the bow in order to set up a firing position in a natural emplacement ten meters away. Sandlin, ready to go, was given a rifle and carried to this frontal position thereby supplying additional firepower.

Concussion grenades were also used to supplement these basic weapons in the forty-minute effort to ward off any attempts of an enemy assault. The foliage proved indeed provident, absorbing much of the enemy fire while precluding his use of rockets and heavy rounds altogether. Though continuous, the resulting incoming fire was relatively ineffective. Only Ruiz was seriously wounded in the ground action as a Chinese hand grenade exploded next to his M-60 firing position. Heroic acts became well-nigh routine as 43 was transformed into a blazing bunker. Some fired while Hinson passed ammunition and loaded M-16 magazines. Weapons jammed and were replaced. Hand grenades were exchanged

with the enemy. But twenty meters away, a diabolical chess game was being played, one Viet Cong spider hole checkmated by Lowry's accurate throw. As a result of this aggressive perimeter action, the necessary volume of fire was sustained and the enemy never risked a frontal onslaught.

Thoughts gravitated toward rescue. Where in almighty hell were the other boats? 43's radio was destroyed beyond repair and the backup PRC-25 unit set up by Lt. Lomas and the SEALORDS staff officer lacked the transmission power to break into the net already fraught with urgent traffic. PCF 38, seventh boat in the file, was just heading out of 43's sight when she realized her trailing sister was missing. Brazenly, she attempted to implement rescue by re-entering the ambush site. Thirty-eight's bravery was thwarted by a rocket round which slammed into her pilot house, severely wounding the OIC and rendering her steering useless. The coxswain's skillful manipulation of the twin screw throttles enabled the boat to limp out of the kill zone without suffering further damage.

Upon reaching the medevac area, 38 passed the word of distress, thereby galvanizing the command boat, PCF 31, and a cohort, PCF 5, into swift action. Both boats entered the kill zone with guns roaring and arrived intact at the scene of battle. Thirty-one maneuvered into a position adjacent to the wreckage while 5 poured out covering fire. Long prayed-for extraction became a euphoric reality as dead and wounded persons were passed up, and finally, the perimeter was withdrawn, exhausted and unbelieving. The evacuation completed, 31 and 5 raced to the medevac perimeter where the dazed men of 43 joined the sombre procession, ferrying the wounded to the dustoff helicopters, vainly trying to collect and convey their thoughts of the past hour. The air was heavy with a pungent haze of disbelief.

Meanwhile, only twenty minutes after her crew and UDT had been evacuated, 43's fate was sealed as over a thousand pounds of high explosives and mortar rounds concocted an eruption of cataclysmic intensity, hurling a spuming vortex of flame, smoke, and twisting metal over five hundred feet into the air. Her twin diesels, which could not be halted during the fight, had overheated and ignited fuel, thus starting the irrevocable chain that ended in her ultimate destruction.

Wisely, the boats refused to risk a night transit and bivouacked in the river, tethering to mangrove stumps within the reinforced defense perimeter. Few of the 43 boat's survivors could muster the strength to close their eyes. Frozen to the decks of their new homes, they gazed into the starry firmament, wondering, reckoning...

…First light of 13 April manifested typical magnificence. Lacking, however, were contemplative spirits necessary for the breathing in of such grandeur. Following the sumptuousness of mawkish tomato juice and canned scrambled eggs, orders were barked and the perimeter troops reembarked in order to proceed with the day's schedule of sweeps. The buzzing activity provided a well-needed elixir, forcing wretched visions of the previous day's ambush into realms of temporary obscurity. Toward nightfall, the sweeps terminated and the Marines formed protective enclaves for the night's rest. The swiftboats, released from support duty, then formed the classic file and headed to sea and safety, retracing the path of the tragic twelfth.

Short minutes after getting under way, the boats passed the still-life remains of the 43, an aesthetic aberration suspended on the north bank of the Duong Keo, simply out of joint with her surroundings. Looking at her bow, bending toward the azure heavens in a searching gesture, one could almost feel motion, a groping for the malignancy which was the cause of her agonizing death. The uninitiated might further try to recreate the essence of the once-pulsating holocaust which presently stood calmly before them. The vibrant sensations of that enormity—the anguish, the torments, the frustrations, and the ecstasy—however, will forever remain an esoteric fact, privy to the surviving fifteen. No effort of meditation could possibly reveal those secrets.

By
Ltjg Peter N. Upton

PCF-22 IS SUNK IN THE DUONG KEO
as
LIGHTNING STRIKES TWICE

On May 5th 1969, with memories of the devastating 43 ambush still fresh, the Duong Keo River once again clamped her jaws into a Sealords PCF unit. Two Viet Cong rockets, fired from north bank emplacements, tore into the aluminum-foil skin of PCF-22, forcing her to beach within hailing distance of PCF-43's mangled wreckage. Two of the four embarked UDT personnel received minor wounds, HM2 Myers suffering a painful broken eardrum and QM3 Broderick, a grazed left forearm. After nine hours of patching and pumping, conducted under the cover of air strikes and troop sweeps, the 22 boat was refloated and towed to sea for permanent repair work.

A mercenary force ground sweep of the enemy trench and bunker positions uncovered a jammed M-60 machine gun, the selfsame weapon, ironically, abandoned by UDT during the 43 battle. QM3 Patrick Broderick relates of this adventure from his unique position, being the only UDT participant in both Duong Keo incidences.

*   *   *

Saturday, 5 May 1969, 6 PCFs, 60 Mobile Strike Force mercenary troops, plus Doc Myers, Whitehead, Morterud, and I departed the LST WESTCHESTER COUNTY at 0600 hours, heading for a sweep and destroy mission along the banks of the Duong Keo River. Everyone was especially nervous about this particular river because it was the same river on which the PCF 43 was destroyed in an earlier ambush. But everyone put down their fears, saying it will never happen again; the VC force that set up that ambush had long since left, we thought.

When the boats got to the mouth of the river, a pop-flare went up, warning the boat officers of danger ahead. When the boats were about 500 meters from the wreckage of the 43 boat, the lead swiftboat, PCF-22, on which we were riding, was hit by two B-40 rockets, one exploding directly under Myers' and Whitehead's position, breaking Myers' eardrum and tearing the lips off a Vietnamese engineer sitting next to them. I was grazed in the forearm by a small arms round.

Shrapnel hit the blowers of both engines, killing the starboard engine immediately, and the port engine soon after. Still within small-arms range, the boats beached. The 22 boat was on fire, with all of the UDT demolitions on board. We all jumped off the boat into a field of punji sticks that the VC had set up along the river banks. I could see tracers whizzing past the heads of Morterud and Doc as we ran for cover behind some small mounds of dirt. The boat crews were trying to put out the fire with CO2 fire extinguishers when mortars started coming in. Four rounds landed inside the perimeter we had set up, killing one MSF mercenary. We were still taking sporadic small-arms fire, which seemed to increase when Doc Myers ran to the boats to patch up the wounded.

The four of us were on the left flank of the perimeter. We knew where the VC were but couldn't see them. The boats mortared the VC positions and put 50-cal machine gun fire on them. We put M-79 and M-16 fire in. We received small arms fire off and on for the rest of the day. The mercenaries were inserted in the ambush position; Navy SEAWOLVES and fixed-wing aircraft with napalm and 500-pound bombs were called in for air strikes while 22 boat was being salvaged. Not knowing whether the 22 could be refloated before dark, UDT rigged demolition charges, in case the boat had to be abandoned and blown up. The 22 had sunk, but was in water shallow enough that it could be patched and refloated. Helicopters brought in pumps, and nine hours later the 22 was refloated and towed out to the nearest ship, a Coast Guard Cutter, by two other swiftboats. UDT climbed aboard another boat and headed to sea, very tired, hungry, and happy to go home, but unhappy that we didn't get to blow up the 22.

By
QM3 Patrick Broderick

REFLECTIONS

Hang yourself, brave Crillon;
We fought at Arques and you
Were not there.

OLONGAPO CITY—a radiant jungle of shimmering neon and sparkling San Miguel beer, where some of us lost our troubles, others lost our money, and still others, that elusive "two-for-one" pay on the slot machine, the cherry.

NO KIDDING—SO YOU LOVE ME AND ALL YOU WANT IS FOR ME TO BUY YOU A HELOCOPTER—WHAT EVER HAPPENED TO FREE LUV?

CONVERSATION OVERHEARD IN THE SUPER CLUB, OLONGAPO CITY

GIRL: "HEY, YOU STATION HEER?"
FROG: "YUP"
GIRL: "WHAT SHEEP YOU ON?"
FROG: "NO SHIP"
GIRL: "YOU ARE MAH-REEN"
FROG: "NOPE, UDT"
GIRL: "U DITTEE...WOT IS THUT?"
FROG: "UNDERWATER DEMOLITION TEAM"
GIRL: "WHAR EES YOU GARLFREN?"
FROG: "I DON'T HAVE ONE"
GIRL: "YOU WAN ME TO BE YOU GARLFREN?"
FROG: "NOPE"
GIRL: "YOU BUY ME DREENK?"
FROG: "NOPE, CAN'T SEE IT"
GIRL: "WHAT EES YOU NAM?"
FROG: "HERM ROID"
GIRL: "MY NAME EES YOLY. WHY YOU NO BUY ME DREENK?"
FROG: "NOW LOOK HERE, I CERTAINLY WON'T PAY FIVE PESOS FOR A GLASS OF TEA. IF YOU WANT A DRINK GO HIT SOME FLEET SAILOR. HE'LL BUY YOU ONE."
GIRL: "WOTTSAMATTER YOU NO LIKE ME?"
FROG: "I'M CONCERNED OVER THE GOLD OUT-FLOW; NOTHING PERSONAL."
GIRL: "I THEENK I GO SEET WEETH THUT BOSUN MATE OVER THAR."
FROG: "BYE"

While we slept that moonlit June night, the USS FRANK E. EVANS collided with an Australian carrier while on maneuvers south of the Philippines. The EVANS was split in two with the resultant loss of 74 Navymen. Our silent thoughts expressed the grief we felt that day.

The stern section of the destroyer USS *FRANK E. EVANS* rests in dry dock at Subic.

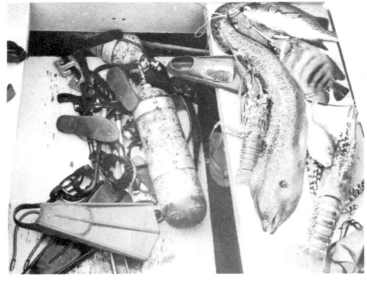

RTTEZYYY RUMUGKD1071 1230641-EEEE-RUMWUAA.
ZNY EEEEE ZFD
R 030641Z MAY 69
FM COMNAVFORV
TO RHMCSDK/CTG ONE ONE FIVE PT FOUR
INFO RUMLPAA/CTF ONE ONE FIVE
RUMUGKF/CO UDT-13
BT
UNCLAS E F T O
CTG 115.4 PASS TO LT LOMAS
A.A. CTF 115 011809X9 APR 69
1. REF A NOTED WITH PLEASURE. THE PERFORMANCE OF YOU AND YOUR MEN
IN SILENT SENTINEL, SEALORDS AND SILVER MACE II IS INDICATIVE OF THE
HIGH STANDARDS OF LEADERSHIP PREVAILING IN YOUR ORGANIZATION.
2. WELL DONE. VADM ZUMAWALT
BT

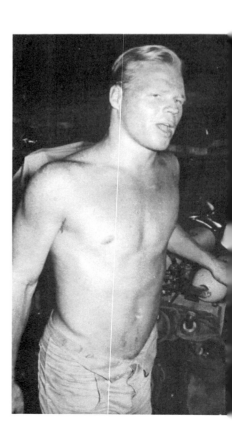

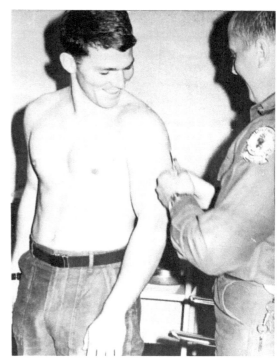

PTTCZYUW RHMCSDP1223 1451433-CCC—RUMMWUA.
ZNY CCCCC ZOV RHMCSDP REROUTE OF RHMCSAA4656 1440800
RUMMWUA ZXY 5
RHMCSAA ZFH 2
R 240800Z MAY 69
FM CTU SEVEN SIX PT ZERO PT THREE
TO ZEN/CTE SEVEN SIX PT ZERO PT SIX PT TWO BRAVO
INFO RUHGSII/CTF SEVEN SIX
RUHGSII/COMPHIBRON THREE
RUAODMA/CTU SEVEN SIX PT ZERO PT SIX
RHMCSDP/CTE SEVEN SIX PT ZERO PT SIX PT TWO
BT
UNCLAS
UDT 13 DET B PERFORMANCE
1. ON THE OCCASION OF YOUR DEPARTURE AFTER NEARLY THREE MONTHS OF
CLOSE ASSOCIATION, I AM MOVED TO EXPRESS MY SINCERE APPRECIATION FOR
YOUR EFFORTS.
2. THE ATTITUDE AND READINESS OF YOUR DETACHMENT TO TACKLE ANY
ASSIGNMENT WITH SPEED AND ACCURACY, COUPLED WITH THEIR WILLINGNESS
TO WORK UNDER LESS THAN FAVORABLE CONDITIONS, ALMOST ALWAYS UNDER
THREAT OF HOSTILE FIRE, PERMITTED THIS TASK UNIT TO MEET EVERY COMMITMENT
DURING YOUR TENURE ABOARD. WELL DONE.
3. YOU HAVE BEEN OUTSTANDING SHIPMATES. GOOD LUCK ON FUTURE
ASSIGNMENTS. SIGNED,
LCDR BRUCE A. TAGER, USN.
BT

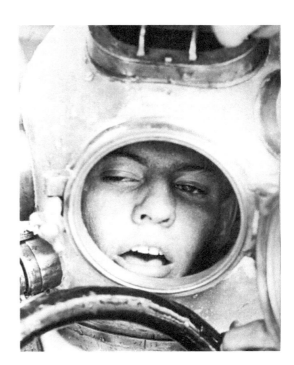

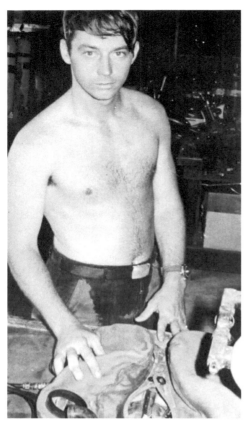

"A small step for a man.
A giant step forward for mankind"

As our prayers were extended during the EVANS' tragedy, our cheers accompanied astronauts Armstrong, Aldrin, and Collins on their historic journey aboard Apollo 11 to the moon. Out of the lunar module 'Eagle' stepped Armstrong, the flight commander, chosen to become the first man on the moon. The mission and the words first spoken on our satellite take an honored place in the heritage of America.

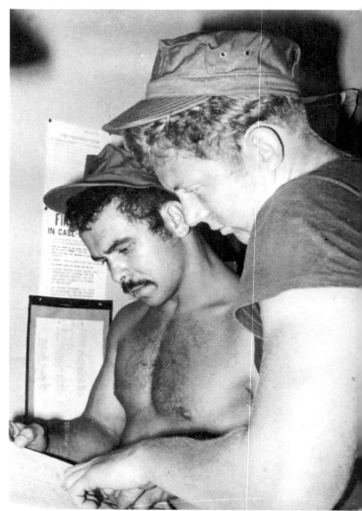

"If you don't speak English, how will we ever get this operation underway?"—E01 Nelson

SEALORDS—moments of alternating despair and exaltation that made you feel 100% alive—the choking agony accompanying your first glimpse of a fallen compatriot; the inner warmth you felt rendering him aid, easing his pain. The tension-ridden, helpless frustration you knew on river transits, counting the thumps of your heart, knowing rockets and bullets were probably aimed your way; the unique spiritual camaraderie which united men under fire.

Moments you devoured, moments you regurgitated, but moments which dug into the very fibre of your existence. Moments fraught with both potency and meaning, instilling your challenges, molding your beliefs, creating your destiny.

*From birth man carries the weight
of gravity on his shoulders. He
is bolted to the earth. But man
has only to sink beneath the surface,
and he is free. Buoyed by water
he can fly in any direction—up, down,
sideways—by merely flipping his hand.
Underwater, man becomes an archangel.*
—Jacques-yves Cousteau

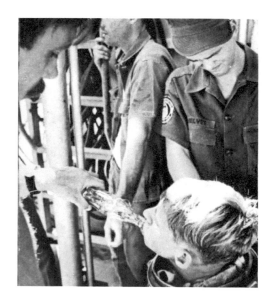

WHEN I REMEMBER THE DOC,
I THINK OF THIS
A song for peace he often sung;
Softly then, but just begun.
Rekindle,
     Like dying embers of love's first night
     In fragrance wafted at dawn's pale light,
And glow renewed in warmth and longing.
                        P.N.U.

Although wars may be fought with weapons and machines, they are won by men. It is the spirit of the man who follows and the will of those who lead that gains the victory.

—G. Patton

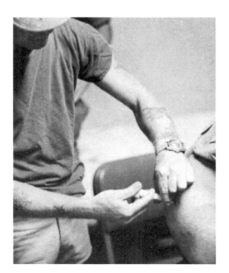

How old, yet ever fresh is the sea;
How constant, yet always changing.
How reliable, yet so restless.
How great its rewards;
How infinite its possibilities.

"Whenever Neal's at the staff meeting, route the correspondence through me." —Ltjg Upton

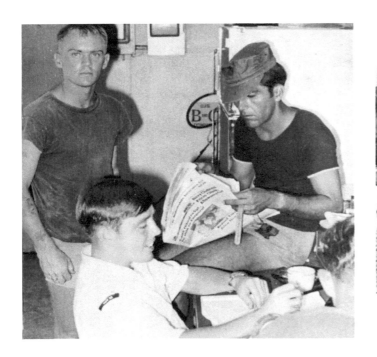

Take a man
12,000 miles from home.
All alone.
Against the odds.
Empty his heart of all
But blood.
Make him live in
Sweat and mud.
There is nothing else
For me to do
But think—
I am supposed to die—
For you.

—S. M. Neal

82

**UNDERWATER DEMOLITION TEAM THIRTEEN
WOUNDED IN ACTION**

LTJG PETER N. UPTON

LTJG JOHN P. WIGGIN

HM2 JAMES W. MEYERS

GMG3 RICKEY G. HINSON

QM3 PATRICK E. BRODERICK

SM3 ROBERT J. LOWRY

SM3 ART "R" RUIZ

SN MICHAEL D. SANDLIN

SN WILLIAM R. PIPER

SA RONALD J. KOZLOWSKI

FROM THE EDITORS

We wish to extend our sincere thanks to the following team personnel for their valuable contributions to the fabric of this cruisebook: Lt. Paul Plumb, Ltjg William Robertson, Ltjg John Wiggin, Ltjg George Green, Ltjg Ernest Jahncke, MMC Terry Manley, ADJ2 Stanley Neal, Seaman Mike Sandlin, SM3 John Lowry, QM3 Patrick Broderick, SFM2 Stephen Freed, Seaman Stephen Abney, Seaman Walter Dudley, Seaman Peter Carolan, Airman Mark Buland, and SA Brian Gillen. Those who offered friendly suggestions are too numerous to name.

We also acknowledge with pleasure the photographic contributions of Captain Gerald Fox, First Special Forces at Camp Hardy, Okinawa, and PHC Arthur Hill of Naval Forces, Vietnam.

*   *   *

The 1969 UDT THIRTEEN Cruisebook brings together a collection of firsthand textual and photographic impressions of our WESTPAC deployment. The harmonizing of these significant experiences, each unique in attitude and point of view, we feel, best conveys the reality of the deployment, to be relived and enjoyed by you in all its color, drama, and poignancy in the years to come.

Ltjg Peter N. Upton

PH1 Steve Waterman

www.ingramcontent.com/pod-product-compliance
Lightning Source LLC
Chambersburg PA
CBHW041420050326
40689CB00002B/591